TIMELINE OF PAUL CÉZANNE'S LIFE

1839 Paul Cézanne is born in Aix-en-Provence.

1844 Paul attends elementary school in Aix.

1857 Paul begins taking drawing lessons at the local free drawing school.

1859 Even though Paul is more interested in art, he agrees to attend law school to please his father.

1861 Paul quits law school and goes to Paris to study art. He returns to Aix to work in his father's bank for a while. Paul eventually gets his father's approval to study art. At the Suisse Academy of Art in Paris, Paul meets many soon-to-be famous Impressionist artists, including Camille Pissarro, Claude Monet, Pierre Auguste Renoir, and Alfred Sisley.

1869 Paul Cézanne meets Hortense Fiquet, a part-time artists' model who will eventually become his wife.

THIS WAY 👉

UP HERE 👆

1872 Cézanne works on improving his work. He sometimes works alongside Camille Pissarro and gets advice from him. Paul and Hortense's son is born.

1874 The first Impressionist show opens in Paris. Paul Cézanne exhibits three of his paintings.

1876 Over the next nine years, Paul Cézanne travels to scenic spots all over France. In some areas, he spends months at a time painting.

1886 Cézanne's father dies, leaving Paul an inheritance. Now Paul can spend all his time painting and can care for his family without worrying about money.

1895 Well-known Paris art dealer Ambroise Vollard gives Paul his first one-man show.

1902 Cézanne has a large studio and house built just outside of Aix.

1906 While painting in an open field, Paul is caught in a heavy rainstorm. He hadn't been feeling well, and now, cold and wet, his condition becomes worse. Sadly, he dies a week later at the age of 67.

GETTING TO KNOW THE WORLD'S GREATEST ARTISTS

P A U L
CÉZANNE

WRITTEN AND ILLUSTRATED BY MIKE VENEZIA

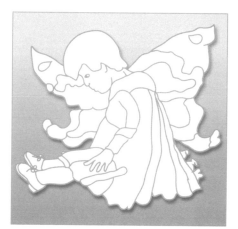

This book was made possible by the
Rosetta Froug Mulmed
Book Fund
established in her memory.

tulsa
LIBRARY TRUST

To Carol Ritzmann Leonard. Thanks for sharing your knowledge of Cézanne. It made this book a pleasure to write.

Cover: *Apples and Oranges*. c. 1895-1900. Oil on canvas, 74 x 93 cm. Musee d'Orsay, Paris, France/Erich Lessing/Art Resource, NY

Library of Congress Cataloging-in-Publication Data

Names: Venezia, Mike, author, illustrator.
Title: Paul Cézanne / Written and illustrated by Mike Venezia.
Description: Revised Edition. | New York : Children's Press, 2016. | Series:
    Getting to know the worlds' greatest artists | Includes bibliographical
    references and index.
Identifiers: LCCN 2015036563| ISBN 9780531216699 (library binding : alk.
    paper) | ISBN 9780531221082 (pbk. : alk. paper)
Subjects: LCSH: Cézanne, Paul, 1839-1906–Juvenile literature. |
    Painters–France–Biography–Juvenile literature.
Classification: LCC ND553.C33 V37 2016 | DDC 759.4–dc23 LC record available
at http://lccn.loc.gov/2015036563

No part of this publication may be reproduced in whole or in part, or stored in a retrieval system, or transmitted in any form or by any means, electronic, mechanical, photocopying, recording, or otherwise, without written permission of the publisher. For information regarding permission, write to Scholastic Inc., 557 Broadway, New York, NY 10012.

©2016 by Mike Venezia Inc.

All rights reserved.
Published in 2016 by Children's Press, an imprint of Scholastic Inc.
Printed in the United States of America   113

SCHOLASTIC, CHILDREN'S PRESS, and associated logos are trademarks and/or registered trademarks of Scholastic Inc.

1 2 3 4 5 6 7 8 9 10 R 25 24 23 22 21 20 19 18 17 16

Self-Portrait with Palette,
by Paul Cézanne. 1885-87.
Oil on canvas. 130 x 97 cm.
Collection E.G. Buehrle,
Zurich, Switzerland.
Photograph © Erich
Lessing/Art Resource.

Paul Cézanne was born in the quiet
southern French town of Aix-en-Provence
in 1839. To show his love for nature,
he painted things in a way that had never
been seen before. Paul Cézanne shocked
people with his new ideas and changed
the history of art forever!

One reason people were shocked with Paul Cézanne's art was that they thought his paintings looked too flat. They were used to paintings that showed lots of perspective —the feeling of distance and space—like in the painting below.

A View near Volterra, by Jean-Baptist-Camille Corot. 1838. Oil on canvas. 27 3/8 x 37 1/2 cm.
Photograph by Bob Grove, © National Gallery of Art, Washington. D.C., Chester Dale Collection.

Mont Sainte Victoire Seen from the Bibemus Quarry, by Paul Cézanne. c.1897. Oil on canvas. 65.1 x 80 cm. © Baltimore Museum of Art, the Cone Collection, formed by Dr. Claribel Cone and Miss Etta Cone of Baltimore, Maryland.

Paul thought that since the surface of a painting was flat, it made sense to paint objects so that they fit better on a flat surface. He didn't think perspective was always necessary to show the beauty of nature.

Still-Life with Fruit Basket, by Paul Cézanne. 1888-90. Oil on canvas. 65 x 81 cm.
Musee d'Orsay, Paris, France. Photograph © Erich Lessing/Art Resource.

Sometimes Paul would show several different views in one painting! In *Still Life with Fruit Basket*, you can see the side of the fruit basket at the same time you're looking at the top of the ginger jar next to it.

The left part of the table is lower and more tilted than the right side. Paul Cézanne did this to make your eyes move from the front to the back and all around the painting as a way of giving it depth without using a lot of perspective.

Paul also used lots of color, building up shapes and objects to make them feel solid. In some of his paintings, even the people seem like they're chiseled out of stone or carved out of clay. Using colors this way was another new idea of Paul's.

The Card Players, by Paul Cézanne. Oil on canvas. 65.4 x 81.9 cm. © The Metropolitan Museum of Art, Bequest of Stephen C. Clark.

9

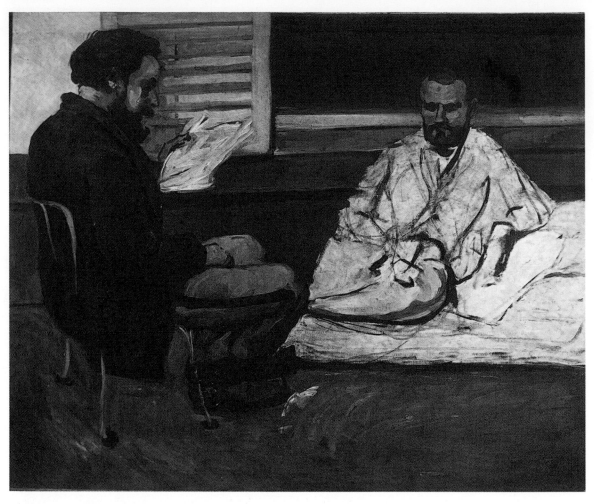

Paul Alexis Reading to Emile Zola., by Paul Cézanne. 1869-70. Oil on canvas.
131 x 161 cm. Museu de Arte, Sao Paulo, Brazil. Photograph © Art Resource.

Paul Cézanne came from a wealthy family. His father owned a bank and was very strict. Paul had only a few friends while he was growing up. His best friend was Emile Zola. Emile became a great author when he grew up. Paul and Emile would spend hours in the countryside around Aix-en-Provence.

They both loved nature. Paul Cézanne never forgot the days he spent picnicking, swimming in streams, and climbing mountains with Emile. They enjoyed reciting their favorite poems under the forest trees. Paul and Emile talked about becoming artists and writers and encouraged each other throughout their lives.

The Artist's Father, by Paul Cézanne. 1866.
Oil on canvas. 78 1/8 x 47 cm. © National Gallery of Art,
Washington, D.C.

Paul never got much encouragement from his father, though. When Paul finished high school and decided he wanted to be an artist, Mr. Cézanne gave him a hard time about his decision. He wanted his son to be a lawyer or work in his bank.

The Spring, by Paul Cézanne. 1859-62. Fresco wall painting transferred to canvas. 314 x 97 cm. © Musee du Petit Palais, Paris, France/A.K.G., Berlin/Superstock, Inc.

The Autumn, by Paul Cézanne. 1859-62. Fresco wall painting transferred to canvas. 314 x 104 cm. © Musee du Petit Palais, Paris, France/A.K.G., Berlin/Superstock, Inc.

Even though Mr. Cézanne didn't think much of art or artists, he did allow Paul to do his portrait, and even let him paint murals on the walls of their large home.

To please his father, Paul studied law in college and even worked in the bank for a while. He couldn't stand doing either one of those things. Paul really wanted to be an artist. He spent as much of his spare time as he could painting and taking drawing lessons at a local art school. Paul even drew pictures on important bank papers to help pass the time.

Finally, Paul's mother convinced Mr. Cézanne how unhappy their son was, and persuaded him to let Paul go to the city of

Paris, France. Paris was where all the great French artists went to study art and sell their work. Mr. Cézanne finally agreed and even gave Paul a small weekly allowance to live on.

The Oath of the Horatii, by Jacques Louis David. 1784-85. Oil on canvas. 330 x 425 cm. Louvre, Paris, France. Photograph © Giraudon/Art Resource.

When Paul arrived in Paris, he looked for an art studio right away. He found one filled with young artists, most of whom were happy to paint in the accepted style of the day. This style was pretty realistic looking, with dark colors and carefully drawn figures, like in the painting *The Oath of the Horatii.*

Interior with Two Women and a Girl, by Paul Cézanne. 1860-62. Oil on canvas. 57 x 92 cm. Pushkin Museum of Fine Arts, Moscow. Photograph © Scala/Art Resource.

This was the type of painting that was selected by the yearly Salon show, the most important art show in France. Since Paul wanted his work to get into the Salon show someday, he started out carefully drawing and painting in a realistic way.

The Murder, by Paul Cézanne. 1868. Oil on canvas. 65 x 80 cm. Walker Art Gallery, Liverpool, Great Britain. Photograph © Erich Lessing/Art Resource.

Paul worked hard studying and drawing live models. He also copied paintings of the old master artists in different museums around Paris. But Paul Cézanne was much too imaginative and restless to just keep doing the same old thing. Soon he started painting strange scenes that were dark and sometimes violent.

Even his self portrait shows him looking angry and upset. In fact, Paul *was* angry and upset. Because he was from a small country town and kept to himself a lot, the students in his studio thought he was rude. They made fun of his accent and the way he

Self-portrait, by Paul Cézanne. 1861.
Photograph © Photographie Bulloz.

dressed. No one liked his art, and the Salon rejected his paintings. Paul also knew that his father hoped he would fail, so that he would come back and work at the bank.

Garden, Trees and Flowers, Spring at Pontoise, by Camille Pissaro. 1877. Oil on canvas.
65.5 x 81 cm. Musee d'Orsay, Paris, France. Photograph © Giraudon/Art Resource.

Paul Cézanne was almost ready to give up. Fortunately, there were some art students he met who knew Paul had a special talent. Two of these artists were Claude Monet and Camille Pissarro. They also were looking for new ways to picture things. They told Paul how much more fun it was to paint outdoors than in a dark, stuffy studio.

They showed Paul how they used lots of bright, beautiful colors to show nature. These were new ideas that Paul Cézanne really liked. Paul began spending a lot of time outdoors. He worked side by side with Camille Pissarro, who turned out to be a great teacher.

The Castle of Medan, by Paul Cézanne. Glasgow Art Gallery and Museum/Bridgeman Art Library, London. © INDEX.

The Poppy Field, by Claude Monet. 1873. Oil on canvas. 55 x 65 cm.
Musee d'Orsay, Paris, France. Photograph © Giraudon/Art Resource.

Claude Monet and Camille Pissarro were part of a group of artists who became known as the Impressionists. The Impressionists were interested in capturing a moment of time during the day in their paintings. They used feathery brush strokes and lots of color.

The Impressionists invited Paul to join them in an exhibit they were having. Paul agreed, even though he really didn't paint their way. Paul wanted his artwork to show nature in a more solid, permanent way.

Although Paul Cézanne respected the Impressionists, he thought too many of their paintings were just pretty pictures. He thought his paintings could be much more than that. Paul Cézanne wanted to do more than just depict nature as it looked. He wanted to show how he felt about nature. This was a very exciting new idea in painting, and one that most people didn't understand.

In 1874, Paul entered his painting *The House of the Suicide* in the Impressionists' exhibit. As it turned out, the show was a big flop. People thought the paintings looked unfinished. They didn't like scenes about everyday life as much as those about an important historical event or heroic story. The paintings they disliked the most, though, were Paul Cézanne's!

The House of the Suicide, by Paul Cézanne. 1873. Oil on canvas. 55 x 66 cm.
Musee d'Orsay, Paris, France. Photograph © Erich Lessing/Art Resource.

La Montagne Sainte Victoire, by Paul Cézanne. c. 1887. Courtauld Gallery, London/Bridgeman Art Library, London. © Bridgeman Art Library. Reproduction required cleared by BAL.

Paul Cézanne was so insulted that he decided to leave Paris and go back home to paint pictures the way he thought they should be done. Paul no longer cared what anyone thought. He started working harder

Woman with a Coffee Pot, by Paul Cézanne. 1890-95. Oil on canvas. 130 x 97 cm. Musee d'Orsay, Paris, France. Photograph © Giraudon/Art Resource.

than ever to express his deepest feelings, with simple, solid shapes and beautiful colors. It was during this time that Paul Cézanne created his greatest works of art.

The Blue Vase, by Paul Cézanne. 1885-87. Oil on canvas. 61 x 50 cm. Musee d'Orsay, Paris, France. Photograph © Erich Lessing/Art Resource.

Ambroise Vollard,
by Paul Cézanne. 1899.
Oil on canvas. 100 x 81 cm.
Musee du Petit Palais,
Paris, France. Photograph
© Giraudon/Art Resource.

    Paul Cézanne always worked very slowly and carefully. He made his art dealer, Ambroise Vollard, sit 115 times for the portrait above! Paul insisted that Ambroise sit perfectly still, and had a fit if he moved even an inch.

By this time, Paul had gotten married. His wife was one of his models. Madame Cézanne must have had a lot of patience, because Paul painted 27 pictures of her.

Madame Cézanne in a Yellow Armchair, by Paul Cézanne. 1893-95. Oil on canvas. 80.9 x 64.9 cm. Photograph © The Art Institute of Chicago.

Apples and Pears, by Paul Cézanne. Oil on canvas. 44.8 x 58.7 cm.
The Metropolitan Museum of Art, Bequest of Stephen C. Clark, 1960.

Paul Cézanne gave as much attention to the backgrounds and space around objects in his paintings as he did to the main subject. He wanted every square inch on the surface of his canvas to be as balanced and perfect as possible. Paul spent many years of his life by himself. He even moved away from his wife and son for long periods of time. He didn't want anyone interrupting his work.

During Paul's life, hardly anyone noticed or cared about his paintings. Only a few people, including Claude Monet, Pierre Auguste Renoir, Camille Pissarro, Pablo Picasso, Henri Matisse, Vincent van Gogh, and Paul Gauguin, realized what an important artist Paul was. Many of these soon-to-be-famous artists felt that Paul Cézanne may have been the greatest of them all.

The Bathers, by Paul Cézanne. 1899-1904. Oil on canvas. 51.3 x 61.7 cm. Photograph © The Art Institute of Chicago.

Self Portrait, by Paul Cézanne. 1875-77. Neue Pinakothek, Munich/Bridgeman Art Gallery, London. © Bridgeman Art Library.

Paul Cézanne died in 1906. His paintings mattered more to him than anything else in the world. He created a new and different kind of beauty in his artwork that influenced almost every modern artist who came after him.

The works of art in this book came from the following museums:

The Art Institute of Chicago
Baltimore Museum of Art
The Louvre, Paris, France
The Metropolitan Museum of Art, New York
Musee de Petit Palais, Paris, France
Musee d'Orsay, Paris, France
Museum of Fine Arts, Boston
National Gallery of Art, Washington, D.C.
Neue Pinakothek, Munich, Germany
Pushkin Museum of Fine Arts, Moscow
Walker Art Gallery, Liverpool, Great Britain

LEARN MORE BY TAKING THE CÉZANNE QUIZ!

(ANSWERS ON THE NEXT PAGE.)

1. **TRUE OR FALSE:** Paul Cézanne often took long trips around the world to find new and interesting scenes to paint.

2. Some of Cézanne's most famous paintings are still lifes of apples, pears, and peaches. But Paul didn't believe any object was ever really still. Why?
- **a** People passing by kept helping themselves to the apples, pears, and peaches he was trying to paint.
- **b** Paul thought of fruits as living things that enjoyed having their portraits painted.
- **c** Paul's housekeeper always moved his tabletop arrangement around whenever she dusted.

3. What was one thing Paul Cézanne couldn't stand?
- **a** Being touched
- **b** Split-pea soup
- **c** Cloudy days

4. Paul Cézanne loved all kinds of delicious French meals. Above all, though, he said his favorite dish was:
- **a** French pizza topped with snails and Camembert cheese
- **b** Popcorn shrimp
- **c** Potatoes cooked in olive oil

5. Why did artist Henri Matisse say "Cézanne is the father of us all."?
- **a** Because he thought Cézanne was his father.
- **b** He was misquoted by a local newspaper reporter. What he actually said was "Cézanne is the father of his son, Paul."
- **c** To compliment and honor Cézanne.

6. What did Paul Cézanne consider to be the most important part of his painting?
- **a** The color
- **b** His brushstrokes
- **c** The composition
- **d** All the above

ANSWERS

1. **FALSE** Paul Cézanne found all he needed near his home in Aix, around Paris, and in many small French villages. He never felt a need to travel the world.

2. **b** Paul felt that even still objects like fruit, led a full life! The way fruits changed colors when they were ripening, their shifting shadows, reflections, and aroma made them seem alive to Paul. He once told a visitor about the fruit he was painting: "They like to have their portraits painted…"

3. **a** Paul hated being touched by anyone, even if they were trying to help him. Once, after Paul tripped and fell down, an artist friend tried to help him up. Cézanne had a fit, ran into his studio, and slammed the door! He was very touchy about being touched.

4. **c** Madame Cézanne was an excellent cook and prepared all kinds of dishes that her husband enjoyed. These included fennel soup, chicken pates, bouillabaisse, creamed codfish, and candied apricots. But if Paul had to choose one favorite dish, he said it would be potatoes cooked in olive oil.

5. **c** Matisse loved and admired Cézanne and his work. He felt Cézanne created the beginning of a new style of painting that influenced almost every modern artist who came after him. He and other artists of the time felt Cézanne was the father of all modern artists.

6. **d** Paul Cézanne would sometimes spend weeks working to get just the right composition, color, and brushstroke for his painting. He felt every dab of paint, shadow, reflection—every square inch of his painting was extremely important.